Time Awareness

for all Musicians

PETER ERSKINE

Cover art: Krzysztof Kokoryn
Back cover photo: Luis de Miguel

ISBN 0-7390-3854-0 (Book and CD)

CONTENTS

Introduction

Life is Rhythm, and Rhythm is Time ... and Music is everywhere around us.

From the smallest molecular organism to the infinite expanse of the cosmos, everything exists in relation to the forward motion and movement of time. And every musical tone, beat, squeak, squawk or bleep exists in time, and in the relationship of itself to its neighboring musical event. Put a couple or more of them together and you'll have some sort of a melody with a discernible rhythm.

It is my experience that most musicians, beginners as well as professionals, tend to take time for granted. Like the air we breathe, it's always there. But, unlike a disciplined athlete or person who practices meditation, most of us inhale and exhale without a true appreciation for the sweetness and power of the air itself. Similarly, a musician who does not appreciate the space of time between the notes that are played is more than likely to cheat the music of its necessary breath.

Some questions:

"What makes a piece of music swing?"
"Should we count as we play?"
"When do I play this next note? In terms of phrasing, should it be 'behind' the beat? 'On' the beat? On 'top' of the beat?"
"Why do some groups sound so 'good' and rhythmically 'right'?"
"Why do we dance to the rhythm of music?"
Time Awareness will attempt to answer these questions.

Okay ... writers like to wax rhapsodic about "Time," myself included. Poets lament how time passes through our fingers, and how we are all but passengers on the boat of life, passing through time, and so on. Enough of that! I propose that musicians begin to think of time the way a football player regards the ball that he or she will carry across the goal line. We are not borrowing the ball, nor is the ball just passing through our hands. We must OWN the ball in order to be successful. Likewise, a musician must feel that he or she OWNS the time when playing music of rhythm.

Suggestion: If you encounter offbeat rhythms and are having difficulty in playing these rhythms, for example:

Imagine how simple it is to play these same notes if they were merely "on the beat," as such:

The most common mistake that musicians will make when playing rhythms is to treat rests (the spaces between the notes) as indeterminate pauses; taking those spaces for granted or guessing their length. REMEMBER: RESTS ARE NOTES, TOO! Silent notes, but every bit as important as the notes you play on your instrument. Each rest should last for its notated duration; no shorter or longer. This one reminder alone should serve you well on your musical journey ... on that boat that is slipping through time, on the sea of life!

There are two types of time awareness that we will focus on: first, our individual sense of feeling and getting the rhythm "right," and second, our ability to play in an ensemble. Both of these have to do with understanding the proper amount of space between each note, and then playing these notes with such conviction that we improve the confidence of the musicians around us.

This book should provide a handy study, practice and resource guide for all musicians who are seeking to improve their music-making abilities. Though I am best known as a drummer, the text, exercises and etudes in this book are not for drummers only! And while a good number of the exercises can be sung or played on any instrument, I suggest and hope that the readers of this book will be encouraged to tap these rhythms out: "playing" your thighs with your hands, for example, will work just fine. The examples can be practiced by yourself, and in duet, trio or quartet combinations. I recommend that you get together with other players in your music ensemble (fellow "section" musicians, for example) to improve your skills.

Please note: The idea is not that musicians should play everything in absolute tempo or with some kind of robotic-like accuracy. Instead, by increasing our sensitivity to rhythm-related matters, we should be able to expand our expressive capabilities to an even higher level of fluidity and poetry.

Foreword

Our hearts beat in time. Ocean waves crest and pound against the shore in time. Birds flap their wings in time. Day and night follow one another in time, and Man has spent the greater part of his existence charting the movement of the planets and the stars. No matter the language, we speak in rhythm and in time.

Music is an expression of our dreams and thoughts. On a more mundane level, music is the sound we coax out of our first drumset, trumpet, piano, or guitar. Music is what we read in the band room at our school during rehearsal. Music is what makes our television shows and movies come alive. Music also seems to be a vital part for the successful operation of every elevator, airplane and place of business! We sing the soundtracks to our lives silently while we walk, or out loud in the shower and car.

Soon after birth, our mothers coo and sing softly to us. We discover the sound of rhythm by tapping our fingers, playing on any available surface with our hands, or by speaking our first sentence.

Each note follows another for the rest of our lives. When we put two or more notes together, we have a piece of music. What happens in the specific timeframe between the notes in any piece of music determines the response of our listeners as well as our own level of satisfaction.

As you play the rhythms in this book, whether by tapping, drumming, blowing or bowing, please remember to **stay relaxed** in both body and mind!!

Have fun making good music.

I. The History of the Drum

In the early 1990s, I was commissioned to write a piece of music titled "The History of the Drum" for the Kokuma Afro-Caribbean Dance Ensemble of Birmingham, England. I proposed a composition that would describe the story of the drum, and, once this was agreed upon by the sponsoring arts council, I realized that a libretto would help me to visualize the rhythmic and tonal construct of the project. I asked my good friend Jack Fletcher, a noted director in theatre and animation, to supply me with a fable of sorts. This is what I got, and I think it describes the first music as well as anything else I've come across:

History of the Drum Track 1

Once a long, long time ago — so long it did not be what long is now. You know. Was a little boy. Did not know there a little girl too.

Somewhere. Probably now we know he looked there for somewhere but we know he asked because he felt that lone. That lone, we know, can feel on globe. Alone. He used to sit and tilt back and lean forth, we know is rocking now and walking then. Boy did he cause he ache and thought the only was he — a bug on a big animal that moved with no of him and so...

He picked up a tiny rock and he threw rock in a lake to make him feel the plunk he heard back from the throwing was nice — he threw another just to hear and see the ripples. Picking up third stone he asked, "so are you part of the animal I live on?"

Stone sat in his hand — he looked and it sat and he stared and so sudden it spoke, "So... you throw me or teeth clicking jaw up and down sound? Why not you just walk now your feet make some ground and you listen cause will they you round." The stone it stop talking the boy start to walk and he walking with step, step, step to this wave, wave, wave to the big water ocean that in and out in a rhythm he loved and he saw on its sand there a girl. There she was rocking self to the wave's voice she loved too.

The waves held their feet and then would let go. The bump found their ears and they sit or could stand. They find that they moved to the come here and go which could sound like slow bird wings or tree crackle winds. Now it would not soon long be they finding their hearts which beat in each two beat and beating in one.

Of course you and me know that this was the start. This was the feet that slammed, and the hands that went to the chest, and the knee, and the wood had the sound that the sticks liked on. Hollow logs told the story strong that logs talked. So did skins that beating spoke like hearts. And men and women and birth and life and feet beating and rocks hitting water meant this life could not end. The stars laugh the shore sigh the heart of globe drum of why.

Originally released by Interworld, the soundtrack recording of *History of the DRUM* is now available from Fuzzy Music at fuzzymusic.com Narrated by Roscoe Lee Browne.

II. The Beat

The Time-Frame

Western music seems to have a fond preference for music that is "even" in metric terms (not "odd"), and that evenness is expressed in music which is conceived and heard in either 4/4 or 2/4.[1]

When we look at the equation of 4/4, this fraction tells us that there are 4 beats to the bar, and each beat is worth a 1/4 of the whole bar (i.e., a "quarter note").

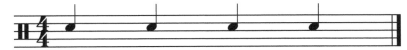

If we play those four notes, over and over, we establish a tempo and a musical pulse. However, there is not much else there to provide inspiration to the listener.[2] What gives a piece of music its own style or identity?

Answer: the subdivision, or underlying rhythmic scheme.

The primary difference between, or defining characteristic of, "jazz" vs. "rock," for example, is the quality of "feel" of the subdivisions of those four quarter notes. In this case, jazz traditionally has a "swung" or triplet feel to the eighth-note subdivisions, while rock has a more straight up-and-down eighth-note feel.

EVERY style of music has its own defining rhythmic scheme. Understanding and interpreting those subdivisions will determine the way our music sounds (or "feels"). Obviously, listening to a style of music (i.e., its feel as determined by the subdivisions) makes our playing of it that much easier and authentic.

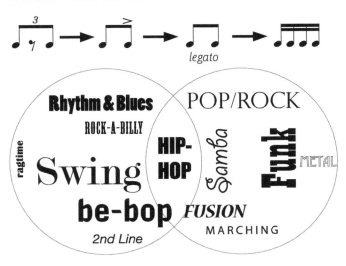

The space between each note constitutes and reflects the subdivision. Where is this subdivision "felt" inside of us?

Gunther Schuller writes in his book "Early Jazz" that, in jazz, the second and fourth beats of a 4/4 measure achieved a form of equality with the other beats of the bar, as opposed to former Western musical traditions where the first beat of the bar was most prominent (especially where the music served the purpose of marching or dancing). And as noted saxophonist and educator Dave Liebman points out, "Eighth notes are the main denomination of jazz time, much like the penny is to the American dollar. Although one may not play only eighth notes, they still serve as the underpinning of jazz time..."

---

1   4/4 can also be expressed in what's known as "cut time" or alla breve.
2   I will define "listener" as being either an audience member or a fellow musician.

EXERCISE #1

Sing the following melody with words, or play it at a piano. Record yourself if possible. Pick any slow-to-medium tempo, but don't use a metronome for now!

Shenandoah

Traditional

Oh, Shen-an-doah,_____ I love your daugh - ter, A - way,_____ you roll-ing riv - er.____ Oh, Shen-an-doah,_____ I love your daugh - ter, A - way,_____ I'm bound a - way, 'cross the wide Mis-sour - i.____

Now, go back and listen to the pickup to measure 3 (the "A" in "Away"), or the second syllable (the "way" in "Away"). Do they fall squarely and comfortably on the downbeat of the measure? Or, was there any "cheating" of the beat? Be honest. (Next measure, too!) Typically, most people, including musicians who are not paying attention, will omit some of the stated rest or space between the notes, especially when crowds of people are singing. (Check out the next person you hear singing "God Bless America" *a cappella*; the chances are excellent that you will notice a few 7/8 or 3/4 bars inserted into the arrangement!)

 Track 2

The accompanying CD to this book contains a relevant and illuminating example. Recently, a young professional saxophonist came to me for lessons, in order to "learn more about time." First, I suggested we play together so I could get to "know" him (included on the CD is an excerpt of an improvisation we did together). As you can hear, he is an accomplished musician. I then asked him to play the following melody for me, without any jazz phrasings or syncopations; in other words, to simply play what was written. As you can see, the melody's rhythm consists of half notes and quarter notes.

I Could Write a Book

Words by Lorenz Hart
Music by Richard Rodgers

I counted off the song (at the metronomic marking of 98 bpm), and he proceeded to play as I recorded his performance. When he was finished, I asked him what he was thinking of while he was playing. He replied that he was thinking of various technical issues like "tonguing," and how to handle the legato phrasings of the notes, etc. Everything but "time," apparently. Still, it sounds okay:

 Track 3

But now, listen to that same performance when a metronome is superimposed upon it:

 Track 4

Different story. Time awareness!

A well-known tune in jazz literature made famous by the Count Basie Big Band is Neal Hefti's "Lil' Darlin'." It is most commonly played at a slow tempo. The rhythmic motif of the melody goes like this:

Lil' Darlin'

NEAL HEFTI

ETC.

It's very hard not to rush this tune, particularly the two quarter notes on beats 3 and 4 that follow the syncopated first note on the "&" of beat one. That dotted quarter note can seem to last a lifetime! I had the pleasure of recording this tune recently with the great jazz singer Kurt Elling. While the Basie Band's famous recording of the tune (circa 1957) resides at approximately quarter note = 66–68 bpm, the newer version of Kurt's (recorded in 2001) rests comfortably at quarter note = 50 bpm.

With or without a metronome, this is a slow tempo! While recording the song, I remember that I was singing eighth-note triplet subdivisions to myself during the entire tune.

Awareness of the music's subdivisions makes it easy to play!

The easiest way to be aware of these subdivisions is to sing them to yourself. This is incredibly helpful, especially at medium or slow tempos. Not only does singing the subdivisions help ensure you're playing with rhythmic accuracy, but also that your performance is stylistically correct. It helps to get you "in the moment." The goal of playing at any tempo is to *own* the time.

For any style of music that you are going to play, listen to a variety of recorded or live performances of that piece or style in order to gain an aural understanding of how that music should be played. Triplets or eighth notes on paper are one thing ... music that is played and brought to life is another!

Chapter III: Our Inner Clock

Time in music is expressed as a tempo.[3]

Once we have set our notes into motion, in *tempo*, we're off and running. Oftentimes we get our tempo from the conductor or leader of the group we're playing in (and oftentimes, of course, the drummer counts off the tune). Other times, we just begin to play at some tempo without really considering how or why ... it simply seems natural.

Whatever the tempo might be once we begin, it is necessary to play our notes in time. This "time" is a sequence of notes in rhythm. Steadiness of the rhythm and overall tempo, as well as authenticity of whatever style we're playing, is **guaranteed** by the awareness and utilization of that music's subdivisions. Steadiness of tempo is also important in most musics!

EXERCISE #2

Record yourself playing any or all of the musical examples in this book WITHOUT a metronome. Begin by counting off the tempo you wish to play. After you have recorded an example, listen back to it with the accompaniment of a metronome that is set to your starting tempo: how well did you stay "on speed"? If you were thinking about anything other than the subdivisions of the beat, the chances are good that your performance strayed from the steady pulse of the metronome (either slowing down or speeding up). Take note of the results, and then try it again. Soon enough, you will sharpen your time awareness when playing alone!

The reader is encouraged to practice the exercises and rhythms in this book at a variety of tempos (e.g., at 60, 90 and 120 bpm). However, in work situations, I have been asked to play at tempos ranging from quarter note = 20 to 320 bpm!

The realm of possible tempos is enormous. To be able to play at any tempo requires CONFIDENCE. The best way to become confident is by EXPERIENCE, and the best way to get experience is to play and PAY ATTENTION to what's going on, musically and otherwise. In other words, CONCENTRATE.

---

3   "Tempo" is an Italian word meaning "time" or movement". Many terms in music come from the Italian language. Musical lexicographer Nicolas Slonimsky continues in his book *Lectionary of Music* "(the) universal meaning in all languages, however, is the musical performance. The marks indicating tempo are also universally Italian: largo, adagio, andante, allegretto, presto and prestissimo. These definitions are often qualified by words of caution such as ma non troppo or poco. The first attempt to put some precise meaning into these vague Italian modifiers was made by the learned German lutist, composer, and theorist, Johann Quantz (1697-1773), who wisely selected the natural human heartbeat of 80 beats per minute as the norm. Taking 4/4 as the basic time signature, he assigned the exact duration of the pulsebeat to a half note in allegro, to a quarter note in allegretto, to an eighth note in adagio. The invention of the metronome, a scientific measurement of tempo, seemed to have standardized this precise terminology. Some particular modern composers, particularly Stravinsky, abandoned the traditional Italian tempo marks altogether and replaced them by the metronome number— his metronome marks were absolute."

Should we count as we play?

Counting is a good way to prevent you from getting "lost" in a printed piece of music, but for feel's sake, I recommend that the musician sing the subdivision to him-or-herself (rather than count numbers). This will ensure that the proper space is left between each note, and will guide the player how to best capture the feel of any type of music. When I sing the subdivisions to myself, I generally sing the offbeat subdivisions. If I'm playing those subdivisions, their realization will reflect my singing/awareness (in other words, it won't just be my hands or feet doing the playing, but my entire musical being). This also helps me "honor" the proper amount of space between each and every note (whether I'm playing them or not)! You should "sing," think or feel the subdivisions in the manner you like best. We will begin by expressing all of the subdivisions as directed below.

Chapter IV: Subdivisions

Elements of Music Review

Reading Rhythmic Notation

A discussion of basic note values and reading musical rhythms is now in order.

Whole - Half - Quarter - Eighth - Sixteenth Notes

The duration of musical sounds (long or short) is indicated by different types of notes.

Whole Note	Half Note	Quarter Note	Eighth Note	Sixteenth Note

One whole note equals two half notes.

One half note equals two quarter notes.

One quarter note equals two eighth notes.

One eighth note equals two sixteenth notes.

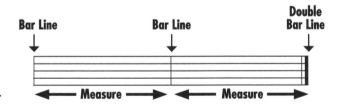

Measure - Bar Lines - Double Bar Lines

Music is divided into equal parts called measures.

Bar Lines indicate the beginning and end of measures.

Double Bar lines, one thick and one thin, show the end of a piece.

Bar Line   **Bar Line**   **Double Bar Line**

◄— Measure —► ◄— Measure —►

Repeat Signs

Two dots placed before a double bar line 𝄇 means to go back to the opposite facing sign 𝄆.

If there is no such sign, then go back to the beginning of the music.

Time Signatures and Note Values

Time Signatures are placed at the beginning of a piece of music. They contain two numbers that show the number of beats (or counts) in each measure and the kind of note that receives one beat.

> **4** = 4 beats to a measure
> **4** = quarter note ♩ gets 1 beat

In 4/4 time, a whole note receives four beats.

A half note receives two beats.

A quarter note receives one beat.

An eighth note receives half of a beat.

A sixteenth note receives ¼ of a beat.

Triplets

A triplet divides the primary pulse into three even subdivisions.

A quarter-note triplet equals one half note: ♩♩♩ = ♩

An eight-note triplet equals one quarter note: ♫♪ = ♩

A sixteenth-note triplet equals one eighth note: ♬ = ♪

In jazz music, the written eight-note pair is most often felt and played as a triplet: ♫ = ♩ ♪

Clef

At the beginning of each line of music there is a clef sign.
Unpitched percussion music uses the neutral (‖) clef.

Tempo

The rate of speed of a musical piece or passage.
Tempo may be indicated by a musical term or by an exact metronome marking.

Metronome

A device which produces clicks and/or light flashes to indicate the tempo of the music.
For instance, ♩ = 120 means that the metronome will click 120 times in a minute and each click will, in this case, represent a quarter note.

EXERCISE #3

Play the following rhythms by tapping them on a desk or table top, or by using your thigh as a drum.
Use a metronome.

First, try to think only of the quarter-note pulse as dictated by the metronome. How easy is it to play in unison with the metronome?

Example A

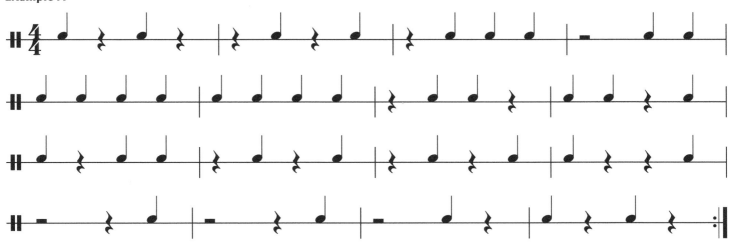

Good ... now let's play those same rhythms with the metronome again, only this time sing offbeat subdivisions to yourself, starting with (straight up-and-down, or "vertical") eighth notes.

Now, "double-up" the metronome tempo (i.e., from quarter note clix to eighth-note clix), and play the same written example. You should find it "easier" to play the rhythms more accurately with this double-time click.

Do the same sequence of events for the following rhythms: first, think of only the quarter-note pulse (i.e., what the metronome is playing), and then play the same rhythms while "doubling-up" the pulse in your head. Follow that with the metronome actually clicking away at twice the speed (i.e., the eighth-note click), etc.

Example B

Repeat the two exercises, but with swung or triplet feel eighth-note off-beats sung between each quarter-note pulse. The same sequence should be applied to the following examples.

Example C

Example D

PLAY EXERCISES AS STRAIGHT-EIGHTHS, AND AGAIN AS 'SWUNG' EIGHTHS, ETC., with the previous sequence of internal and metronomic (click) subdivision variations.

Please listen to "Sideman Bop" on the accompanying CD if you have any questions about the interpretation of the written eighth note as a "swung" eighth (or TRIPLET FEEL), and kindly refer to the next chapter, titled "What makes a piece of music swing?"

 Track 5

Rhythm Etudes C + D now appear in 2/4 time ... the rhythms "sound" the same if the tempo of the 2/4 example is "halved." These sort of "enharmonic" rhythmic exercises are good for sightreading practice, as well as for building your confidence when it comes to seeing a lot of "ink" on a page of music.

Example C2

Example D2

And now, let's take a couple of looks at a tune most everyone knows: "Old MacDonald." Read through and perform these various versions of "Old MacDonald" while changing your inner clock's subdivision awareness ... you should notice a difference in how the melody feels and sounds, depending on how tuned-in your rhythmic radar is. The chances are good that, if you are not subdividing at all, the dotted half note in measure 4 will be cheated of its full and proper length. (7/8 bar, anyone?)

OLD MACDONALD

TRADITIONAL

1.

What makes a piece of music swing?

It will be helpful to discuss some interpretive guidelines for playing written eighth notes in a "swung" manner. My thanks to noted composer, arranger and jazz educator Bob Curnow for allowing me to paraphrase and share his insightful explanation:

"The eighth-note subdivision should be subdivided and felt in three parts (i.e., a triplet) so that when you see a duple rhythm they are interpreted as the first and third parts of an eighth-note triplet.

In other words, the eighth notes on the beat are 2/3 of a beat in duration, and the eighth notes not on the beat are 1/3 of a beat in duration and are played on the last third of the beat.

This rule of triple subdivision must be applied (though it often is not) to all rests within a measure as well as to all notes. A helpful rule to remember is that the first eighth note or eighth rest on the beat is not 1/2 a beat long but rather 2/3 of a beat long."

Saxophonist and educator Dave Liebman puts it this way: "In order to master the subtleties of playing convincing and swinging eighth notes it is necessary to understand various aspects that play a role in their execution. It is important to remember that though there are technical variables which are peculiar to each instrument in the actual playing of eighth notes, the effect is still the same. So though a pianist must, for example, figure out the proper finger movement to articulate eighths compared to a saxophonist's use of the tongue striking a reed or the string player's plucking, the goal is still the same which is well placed eighth notes. It's understood that from the standpoint of being an instrumentalist, each musician must discover and practice the intricacies of execution which are idiosyncratic to their instrument.

Swing has been one of those things that you either "got," or you didn't. There was no way to say, this swings and that doesn't, except for a personal feeling.

No longer. As an article by Mick Hamer in New Scientist explains, swing has now been analyzed scientifically. The basic rhythmic unit in jazz is the quarter note. That's usually what defines the "beat," what you tap your feet to. Melodies are superimposed over the beat, and are often made up of eighth notes, which, in classical music, are exactly one half as long as quarter notes. However, the jazz musician would play those notes alternately long and short, with the long note on the beat, and the short note off the beat. That's the basis of swing, but it's more complicated than that. Making the long eighth note exactly twice as long as the short eighth note, like a drum machine, will make your "jazz" sound mechanical and dull—so Anders Friberg, a physicist at the Royal Institute of Technology in Stockholm, decided to see if he could analyze swing scientifically and see how real musicians play it."

I think we could generalize that a feeling of swing has a drive or momentum in balance with a feeling of relaxation and effortlessness. There is a "lilt" or bounce to the music that is beyond words. It is probably easier to point out what doesn't swing than what does!!"[4]

Here are some rhythmic examples and exercises to help you practice and realize the jazz feel: try these while changing the subdivision undercurrent in your time awareness, e.g., quarter note versus "straight" eighths versus triplets, versus "swung" (*legato*) eighths.

COMMON JAZZ RHYTHMS

7.

8.

9.

10.

MOMENT'S NOTICE RHYTHM

Do you notice any change in the quality of "feel" of these rhythms as you change your subdivision/thinking?
You should (even with the quarter note-only rhythms, however subtle or slight)!

TRIPLET RHYTHMS

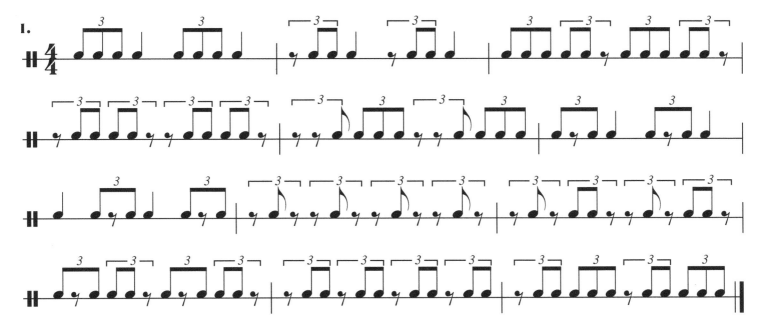

And now, sing offbeat sixteenth-note subdivisions to yourself as you play these basic rhythms.

The Shape of the Note (Phrasing)

Quoting Dave Liebman again, he writes: "Another way to conceptualize articulation is as degrees of intensity in the attack of a note from light to hard, aggressive to gentle and so on. Another consideration is that certain styles of jazz might invoke one form of articulation as more favorable and therefore prevalent for that particular idiom. For example, one aspect of Charlie Parker's innovations in the 1940s was his more legato articulation in combination with a constantly changing continuum between a relaxed and aggressive beat as compared to the earlier swing or dixieland players. John Coltrane's articulation was more legato than the beboppers and so on. As a generalization we could say that the vast majority of articulations heard in jazz fall somewhere between staccato and legato with an incredibly vast palette of variety."

In other words, simply blowing air through your horn and correctly fingering the notes without any regard for phrasing will most likely result in a "flat" and uninspired performance (musically meaningless).

Along with a good teacher to show you the way, listening is one of the best and truest methods to learn proper articulation for any style of music. Pay attention not only to the rhythmic placement, but also to the "envelope" or shape of the note, its articulation, as well as the length of each note.

A common misconception of jazz or swing rhythms is that the triplet feel must *always* be emphasized. However, if you have listened to an improvisor such as Charlie Parker, or the big band writing of Gil Evans, you will have clearly heard that the eighth notes are often played, rhythmically, in a more straight up-and-down manner as opposed to the triplet feel. However, it is the slight accenting of the offbeat eighth note that produces the forward (yet relaxed) momentum and propulsion that is characteristic of good swing ... Mr. Liebman again offers: "The use of an accent translates to a louder note which in turn obviously means what came before and after appears softer. The softest articulated note in jazz is termed interchangeably a ghost, swallowed or muffled tone. This up and down character of dynamics/accents is extremely important to the overall rhythmic feel and is an area where individuality can be clearly discerned."

Sing the following rhythms as written (i.e., unaccented), first, as even eighth notes, then swung and then as even eighth notes with each offbeat eighth note slightly accented. Can you hear and feel the difference? Which way feels best to you?

Sideman Bop

Track 5

Peter Erskine

Practice these phrasing variations with various lead sheets of jazz melodies.

I submit that the best and easiest way to learn how to swing, and to chart or know the difference between what swings and doesn't, is to LISTEN to as much good jazz as you can. Learning the language of jazz by ear will enable you to speak it convincingly!

Chapter V: Ensemble Playing or
When do I play this next note?

Question: How can ensembles play the kinds of various rhythms we've just studied accurately and together?

Answer: By **everyone** thinking of ("singing") the same **subdivisions**.

Whenever I work with bands in high schools or colleges, I find it helpful (as well as necessary) to remind all the musicians that each player in the band is similar to one finger of a giant-handed musical entity who is playing this band like a great big synthesizer. We're all part of one mind and musical impulse when it comes to *tutti*[5] passages.

Another way to put it: every musician must be a drummer, and the drummer must be every musician.

(From an interview with Bob Brookmeyer, October 12, 1999, in *Jazz Improvisation Magazine*)

(Answering the question: "When you were first working with the band, you mentioned you were working with them on playing better; are you referring to articulation and the subtleties of approaching big band arrangements from more of a small group or a jazz feel? What specific things were you working on with them to develop their performance?")

Bob Brookmeyer: "Well, all the jazz bands have the same problem. They play eighth notes much too briefly. They don't give rests, whether it be 8th or whole rests, their proper value. And little things, like the first note of a phrase is the most important note. If the first note of the phrase has the proper weight and proper size, then the rest of the phrase will probably be okay. But almost all bands cheat the first note. It is like they want to get to the last note, and they get to go home early! So that's one thing."

"The producing of eighth notes... I tell them to make it a "doo-waah," so the first note of two eighth notes, instead of "da-dat," is "doo-waah." So, any hints and principles of how to play in a relaxed way and manner that I have learned over the years, and I have learned how to translate them for use in big bands, professional or college."

Interpretive phrasing by the players, in teamwork as a section (trumpets, trombones, woodwinds, rhythm, etc.), results in a blend of rhythmic intention which can otherwise be characterized in most cases as "swing." Swing can be characterized as a forward-moving "horizontal" style of music, that flows effortlessly and with energy all at the same time. If everyone in the group is bouncing along to the same subdivision, chances are pretty good that the band is swinging.

Note: Drummers think of and/or play the notes between the "notes." It is a good idea for keyboard, string and horn players to fill these spaces for themselves as well.

"Classical" musicians, please note: The importance of knowing the difference between "swing" and "straight" note placement pertains not only to jazz and pop musics, but to the great classical literature of the masters as

---

5   The entire instrument section, orchestra, or ensemble.

well. One of my percussion teachers, the late Billy Dorn who played in the NBC Symphony under the baton of Arturo Toscanini, told me the following anecdote: One day at a rehearsal of Beethoven's 7th Symphony, maestro Toscanini stopped the orchestra and, in exasperation at the string players' interpretation of the written dotted eighth- and sixteenth-note patterns in the fourth movement, pounded the sixteenth-note subdivision on his open hand with his baton. The musicians were "swinging" the pattern, that is, playing them "lazily" (in Toscanini's opinion), more as triplets than what Beethoven had written. This same scenario has been repeated in many other ensembles, including (according to a colleague of mine) the Beethovenhalle Orchestra in Bonn, Germany. Even though these players are known for their faithful rendering of Beethoven's music, their occasional lack of subdivision awareness made them fall prey to rhythmic error.

I toured with Joni Mitchell in 2000, and we played with a variety of orchestras that were assembled in major US cities like New York, Boston, San Francisco, Los Angeles, Chicago, Detroit, and so on. Some of these bands were excellent, and some were not-so-great. However, the arranger and conductor, Vince Mendoza, had to say the following admonishment and reminder to every orchestra we worked with: "Subdivide, people! You HAVE to sing the 16th notes to yourself if you're going to play this music correctly …"

So, whether it's Mozart or Mendoza, Beethoven or be-bop, Schubert or shoo-be-doo-be-doo, time awareness counts!

An interesting twist: While writing this book, I chanced upon the great conductor Michael Tilson Thomas in the Café of the Hotel Imperial in Vienna. We sat and spoke about matters musical, and I told him about this book and, specifically, wanted to know his opinion about time and rhythm in the symphony orchestra (and "classical" music in general). He said a couple of things that intrigued me and have great relevance to this discussion. First, while confirming the need for rhythmic awareness and exactness by orchestral players, he pointed out that 1, most classical music is not rendered in a steady tempo as compared to jazz and pop music (tempos are always changing to serve the music), and 2, most of the rhythms that we hear when we listen to classical music might *seem* to be one thing but are, in fact, another. Explaining this statement further, he made an analogy between the Greek Parthenon and music. While the Parthenon[6] *appears* to be constructed in square, the actual *placement* of the columns are in fact inclined, allowing for visual perspective to complete the picture of the columns as standing upright. And so, in music, rhythms can be played one way in order to be perceived in another way. Taking Beethoven's 7th Symphony again, Michael detailed how some of the dotted eighth- and sixteenth-note combinations are actually played with the sixteenth note being articulated "further to the east" (i.e., a bit later and, thus, shorter) than what is written, in order for the ear to better hear the syncopated space between the notes. By the time this effect is multiplied by an entire violin section, it settles into a Beethovian rhythm that we recognize.

Often, rhythmic accuracy is not only a matter of time awareness, but of phrasing execution as well. According to my friend in the Beethovenhalle Orchestra, properly playing the dotted eighth and sixteenth-note combinations in the strings would involve "very little bow—middle to lower half (especially the violas); otherwise tending to triplets."

Another Viennese colleague told me about the late conductor Carlos Kleiber, renowned for his interpretations of Beethoven among others. In order to achieve his desired result of rhythmic phrasing from the Vienna Philharmonic while rehearsing the slow movement of the Beethoven 4th Symphony, he urged the musicians that the rhythm was not "Ma-rie, Ma-rie," but rather "The-rese, The-rese" (referring to Marie Therese Hapsburg, who ruled the Austrian Empire from 1740–1780). In musical terms, Kleiber wanted better

---

6　　The Greeks, who built the Parthenon, studied "Phi", the mathematical phenomenon also known as the "Golden Ratio", "Divine Proportion" or "Golden Mean", which is expressed as AB/CB = CB/AC = 1.618, and is employed in their architecture; it also appears in nature as well as many different kinds of art, including musical composition!

separation between the two notes, with the first (pick-up) note being played shorter and the second note of the phrase played longer. This is a true and charming story.

Beethoven's 7th Symphony Rhythm Examples

Tempo, Note lengths, Counterpoint and Technique:

Fast Tempos

The key to playing fast: keep it light—float—and see the big picture; again, don't be in too much of a hurry. Your engine is most likely strong enough to get you "there" with time and energy to spare! Of course, at a fast tempo it will be nearly impossible to sing the music's subdivisions to yourself. The training you give yourself at slower tempos will strengthen your intolerance for improperly-spaced rests at any tempo. Noted jazz educator Hal Galper recommends that improvisers count or feel the music in "2" (or "cut time"); he submits that this concept will enable the player to phrase in a more swinging manner.

Slow Tempos

The goal when playing at a slow tempo is to not speed up or slow down!

Slow tempos can be challenging, but I think they're a lot of fun. You can really enjoy the musical scenery as it's passing by, and the space in the music gives you a terrific chance to take stock of your sound and touch, as well as your innate sense of time.

When I sing the subdivision of any beat to myself, I will usually not count words or syllables (like "1-e-&-ah, 2-e-&-ah" or "1-trip-let, 2-trip-let"). Instead, I will sing an actual or imaginary musical subdivision to myself, like a rhythm guitar part or a Count Basie Big Band horn section's shout chorus. I am improvising a form of rhythmic counterpoint to everything else that is going on. It's okay to sing whatever you want. The important thing is to honor the spaces between the music's pulses and notes.

The key to playing a ballad: you must not seem in a hurry to get somewhere!

(However: Iilt is a fine line between "relaxed" and (possibly) slowing down: WATCH IT!) In a ballad (or any song, for that matter), there are 2 responsibilities: 1, to the feel and emotion of the song, and 2, to the TIME!

Note Lengths

Whatever the tempo, be aware of note lengths. Whether written long or short, or articulated as your interpretive heart desires, the proper length of a note will help the music feel better. Composers and arrangers are generally quite specific when they notate a particular note length. When playing in an ensemble, the success of a musical passage will depend in great measure to everyone playing the music as written. Sometimes it will be necessary to shorten the length of one note to properly "get" to the next note in time (i.e., the appropriate length of a note can act as a springboard of sorts. The same goes for our silent note friends, rests.).

Proper articulation is a key tool in the musician's toolbox of techniques.

Counterpoint

No matter the tempo, rhythmic counterpoint is an important key to feel — whether expressed (played) or realized internally. In other words, improvising musicians, whether soloists or rhythm section accompanists, should always be composing lines and motifs that complement and counter the melodic lines occurring elsewhere in the music. If you're playing a written part, make it part of the fabric of the music; weave your part into the overall mosaic. By realizing and internalizing such counterpoint creativity and awareness, you give yourself a tremendous tool for reference and inspiration.

Technique

A word about technique: "Technique" is a process, not an end in itself. You'll find that your technique will be constantly evolving. It is important, of course, to have a good foundation on which to build upon. For me, "technique" ultimately means finding the easiest and most natural way to express my ideas on and through the instrument. After many years of playing, I have stopped "fighting" my instrument (the drums), and I've found it to be a good friend. It's all about playing the music, and serving the song.

Duet #1

Duet #2

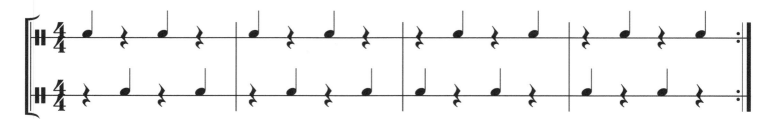

Duet #3

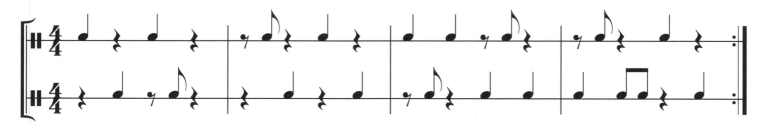

Duet #4

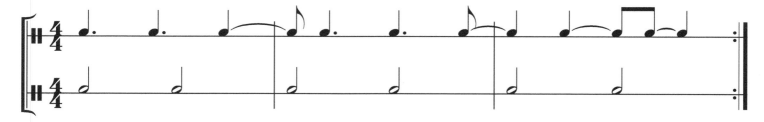

Duet #5

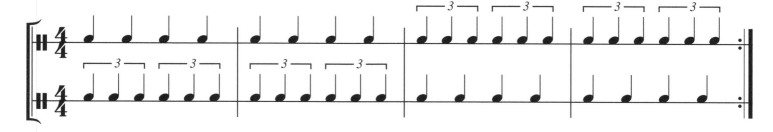

Duet #6

Duet #7

Duet #8

Duet #9

Duet #10

Duet #11

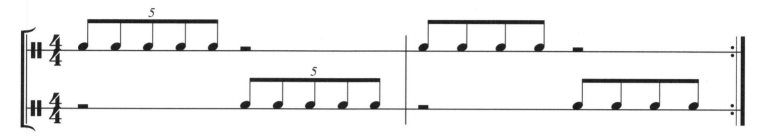

Duet #12

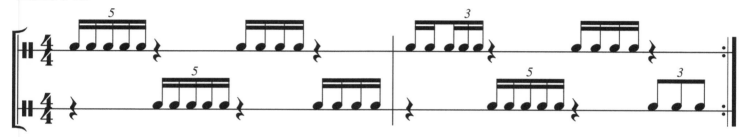

Trio #1

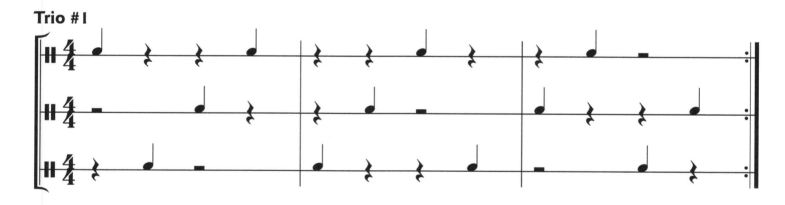

Trio #2

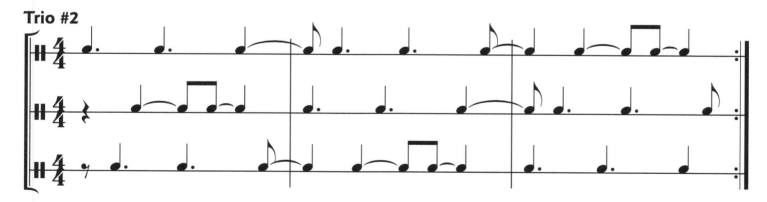

Trio #3

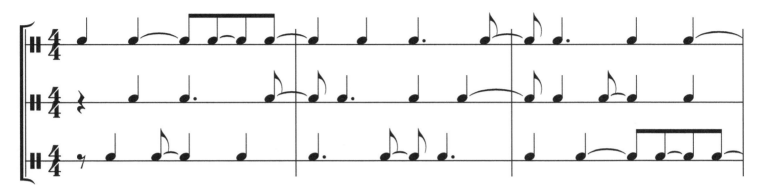

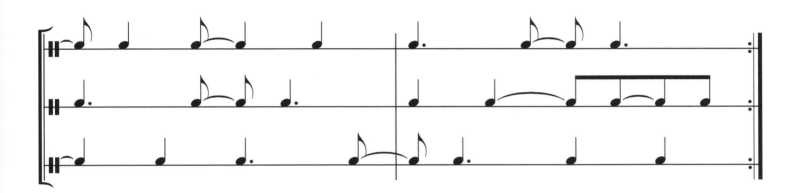

It will become apparent that multiple levels of subdivision awareness are required to best navigate a passage of rhythmically complex music. By combining your training along with your aural skills, you will develop a multilayered understanding of rhythm and phrasing.

Chapter VI: Why do we dance to the rhythm of music?

Reminder: The subdivisions define the style and substance of the music.

Pop or Rock vs. Swing vs. Brazilian or Afro-Caribbean vs. the Viennese Waltz vs. the Concert or Marching Band vs. Hip-Hop or Rap ... the interesting thing is, if we chart the different styles of subdivisions, we can see that not only do many of these styles overlap; quite a few styles have come back around full-circle. And for every style of music which might seem "new," there's a good chance that its rhythmic origins are easy to trace by going back in time!

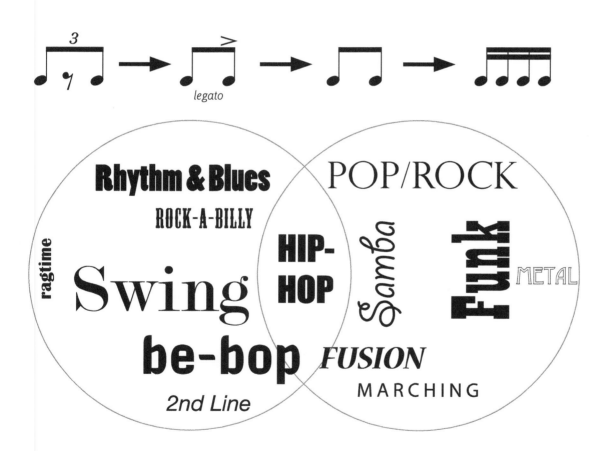

Play the following "Funk & Pop Rhythms" while thinking of, first, only the quarter-note pulse. Then repeat each example thinking of the eighth-note subdivision, the 16th-note subdivision, etc. Finally, play these rhythms while NOT thinking of anything! You should be able to clearly hear and feel the difference.

Funk & Pop Rhythms

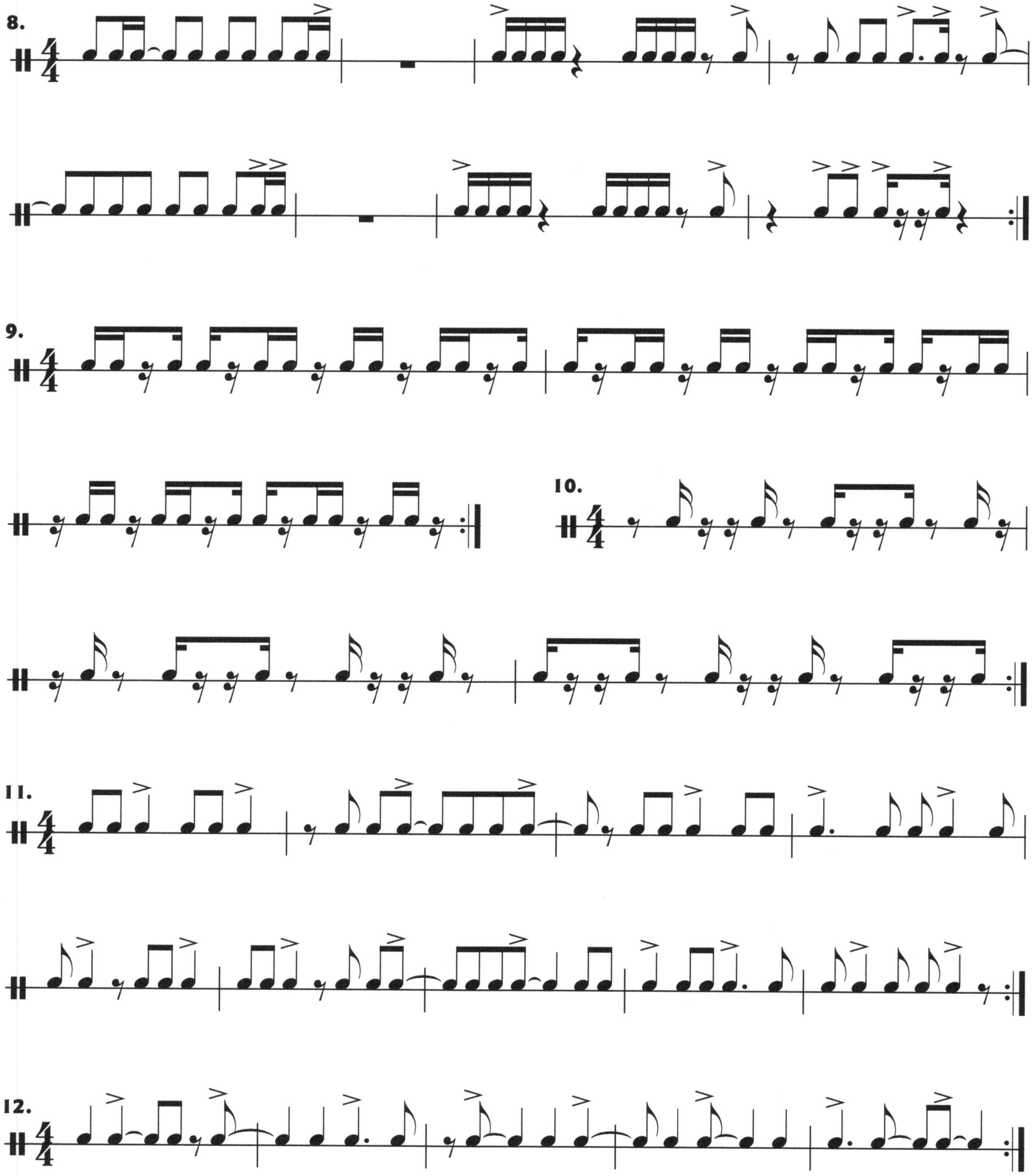
8.
9.
10.
11.
12.

Drumset-Type Rhythms

It's a good idea for every musician to be able to play the piano as well as the drums. Try some of these simple drumset rhythms: the Right Foot/Left Hand examples should be played while the right hand plays each of the following variations. Note: the rhythms can be played "straight" or "swung."

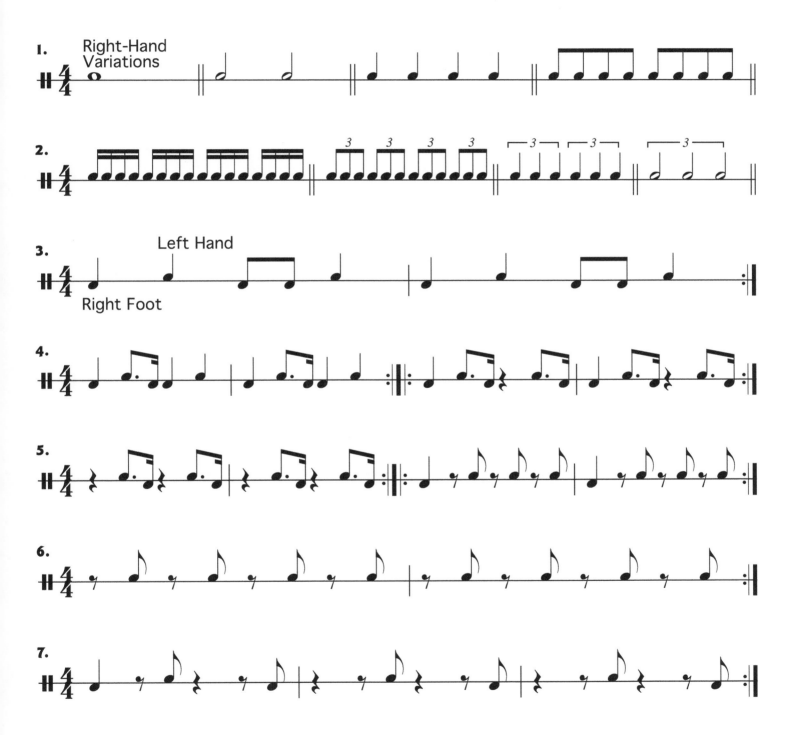

Two-Hand Exercises

1.

2.

3. **4.**

5.

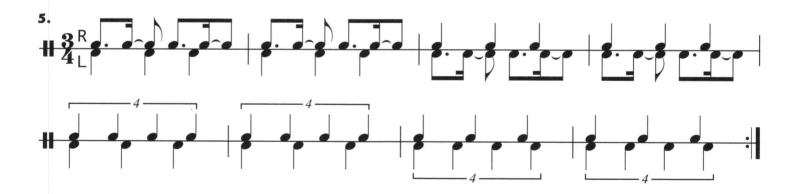

When do I play the next note?
(reprise)

In order to groove, there has to be accurate placement of the beat—not only the pulse, but also the smallest denominator of the subdivision. You have to be aware of that, singing it to yourself as you're playing. If I'm thinking of eighth notes when I'm playing a straight eighth-note beat, it's virtually impossible for my bass drum, snare drum, hi-hat or any part of a fill to be played in the wrong place, out of tempo, out of meter, or out of the groove.

If you play purely from muscle memory, then it's possible (and likely) that your drumming, or performance on any instrument, is not going to swing or groove, and that the placement is going to be inaccurate.

When I (subconsciously) sing the subdivisions to myself, I have established an internal reference point, and everything I play will relate to, and lock onto, that groove. When I sing to myself, I am not counting the subdivisions ("1-e-&-a, 2-e-&-a," etc.), but rather singing an appropriate feeling rhythm part (e.g., a rhythm guitar part). Of course, it is necessary to listen to the rest of the rhythm section in order to be able to play any kind of beat together!

Having a reference point really helps me in my realization of any kind of a beat or performance, whether I'm playing free, playing traditional swing, or playing straight eighth-note musics.

Who and what is 'funky'?

The key to playing funk: Accuracy (subdivide!), with phrasing options (combinations) of playing *staccato*, *detaché* and *legato*.

Two-Person Funk Studies

Musical Rhythm + Improvisation

To play musically, we must respect each note to the fullest. In other words, do not cheat the beat. And, by allowing room for each of your notes to "sing" and for the other instruments in the band to speak, some real dialogue and communication can happen on the bandstand. To me, that's what contemporary music is all about.

Conceptually, one way I think of this is as real-time architecture with a three-dimensional idea of space and placement that provides depth, air and light in the music (as opposed to density). The reference points are vital; the issue is whether or not you fill them up with all these subdivisions when you're playing. One style of playing, which is the way I'm generally trying to play, leaves something to the listener's imagination. It invites the listener in.

When I hear master musicians play, sometimes it's so open and a real surprise because I don't know whether they're going to hit an accent here or an accent there (or a "tonal" or "atonal" note). It's a wonderfully organic blossoming of the music, and the listener can get emotionally involved.

In this way, your ears (and the music) are free to explore and develop any idea to its maximum (or minimum!) potential.

In other words, we allow the music to tell us what to do.

DISCIPLINE YOURSELF. Start with a simple set of note choices to work with. By limiting your rhythmic and tonal choices, you can concentrate on the music you are actually making. Otherwise, the tendency is always to play "licks" or to simply run scales, etc.

How does music make our hearts soar?

"Tell a story."

"Be expressive."

Listen to the phrasing of the written melody by pianist Alan Pasqua on the accompanying CD performance of "Summer's Waltz" while looking at the lead sheet (p.48).

 Track 12

This is an excellent example of bringing the written note to musical life, playing in time, yet applying such phrasing concepts as breathing, *espressivo*, a slight bit of *rubato*, and that most *mysterioso* of musical expression, **swing!** Note, too, the use of dynamics and accents by good musicians.

Above all, however: "To thine own self be true."

What's your time tendency?

Recently, I was working with some talented young musicians who play in one of the local university jazz bands here in Los Angeles. After asking this rhythm section to play several different tempos, I made an observation to the bass player that he might want to begin practicing some basic time feels along with a metronome. This, because I was noticing a tendency that morning for him to slow down as soon as the ensemble began playing. He replied that he was confused, because everyone was telling him that he "always speeds up" when he plays.

How about you? Is your time (ability or propensity to hold tempo) rock steady, or do you tend to speed up or slow down when you play?

Here's my answer: Good time is good time. If you speed up OR slow down, it's natural, it's human, and it might be okay ... but it's not good time. And if you slow down, you're just as apt to speed up, or vice-versa. Any and all players I've encountered whose time is not rock steady will go both ways in the tempo spectrum when their time feel is not settled. Faster and/or slower, it just depends on the circumstance of that particular day or setting.

The effect of the paradox can be heightened when you are playing alongside another musician whose tempo tendencies are known to or have been categorized by you. For example, "I'd better watch it, this player tends to slow down," etc. Oftentimes, the result will be that YOUR playing slows down as well, despite your efforts to push or play ahead of the beat!

Why is this?

Because "good time is good time," and bad time isn't ...! Okay, the more important or practical reason is that:

1. once you are playing and spot-checking/auditing your own note choices or time placement or ...

2. auditing another player's time placement compared to your time placement and then ...

3. asking yourself "is it slowing down?" or "is it rushing?" ...

4. and by the time you've gone through these sorts of mental checklists you've actually paid very little attention to the MUSIC ...

5. and the music and your playing of it become completely "vulnerable" to any external influence ...

6. and it all becomes like trying really hard to say something funny and then wondering why it didn't feel natural (or funny!)...

A. You must "own the time."

B. Recommendation: Practice with a metronome!

Other aspects of time awareness include learning the lengths of groups of measures (or phrases) so you will not need to rely upon counting each measure in a piece of music. Pay attention to song forms. In the case of jazz, song forms often follow rules or a certain standard. Indeed, standards tend to be of A-A-B-A construction. The A section is a part of the melody that's repeated twice, followed by the B section which is the bridge, then A is repeated again. If each section is eight bars long, you have a 32-bar song form. Each 32-bar completion is known as a *chorus*.

STANDARD FORM EXAMPLE

COLE BERLIN

Some songs, however, may have the melody extended the last time through, or a tag at the end of the form. When I play time during a tune, I observe and take note of the song form. If it's not standard, and if there's a four-bar tag or something, I'll make a mental note of that in case I'm going to solo on the form later. Or, the song might be a blues (normally a 12-bar form ["chorus"] that's divided into three four-bar phrases).

Odd Meter Subdivisions, from a Drummer's Point of View

2s + 3s

Most of the music that I have encountered in my drumming life has been in 4/4 meter. Some world musics, like the Brazilian *samba*, are traditionally felt and notated in binary time, or 2/4.[7] The waltz, in 3/4 time, has 3 beats per measure and is familiar to most everyone.[8]

In a jazz waltz, the drummer has the choice of playing the following:

a. The classic "ting ting-a ting" ride pattern:

b. The same ride pattern with the hi-hat on beats 2+3:

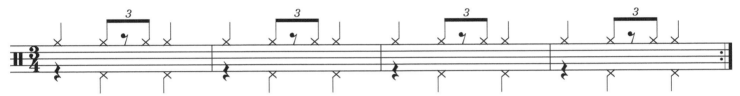

c. The same ride pattern with the hi-hat on all three beats:

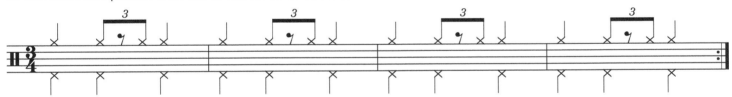

d. The ride pattern with the bass drum playing dotted quarter notes, or a *duple* feel:

e. Adding the hi-hat to that, and extending the ride pattern a bit:

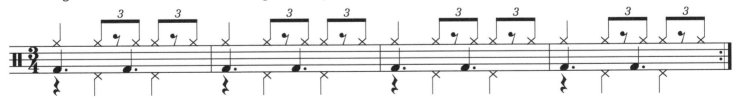

---

7   Prior to the mid-1950s, most of all jazz was in duple meter (with 2 or 4 bears to the bar); the built-in steadiness of such a pulse allowed for the development and use of varieties of syncopation, anticipation, and hemiola-rhythmic devices, especially during the swing and be-bop eras.

8   The use of 3/4 jazz was a novelty at first, notably introduced in 1942 by Fats Waller in his composition "Jitterbug Waltz". Max Roach and Sonny Rollins followed suit in the 1950s by incorporating 3/4, 6/4, and 6/8 into their compositions. Today, jazz music is played in any number of metric settings and most of us are pretty used to it; not so in the early 1960s, when leading jazz educator John Mehegan declared that anything not in 4/4 could not be considered jazz! Dave Brubeck, Stan Kenton, and Don Ellis changed that. Dave Holland's music continues the good fight today.

f. A straight-ahead "walking" 3:

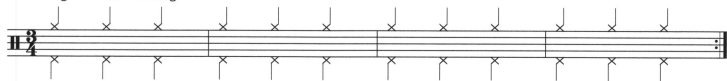

g. The bass drum and snare playing offset duple beats; this is a classic example of a **hemiola**. This type of approach can be employed quite effectively in 4/4 time as well (the snare and bass drum patterns will cross over the barline in that case. Instant Elvin Jones!).

In 3/4 time:

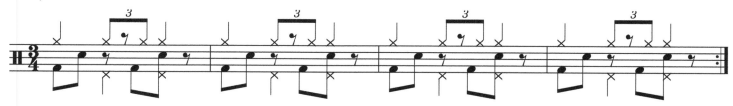

or this variation:

In 4/4 time:

Elvin-ish 3/4 Grooves

Played by
Peter Erskine

Transcribed by
Matt Slocum

Because most of us have repeatedly heard music in 3/4 time ("Happy Birthday," "My Country 'Tis of Thee," the waltzes of Johann Strauss, etc.), it seems like second nature to play in 3/4 time and know where we are in each measure of music. The same, of course, also goes for 2/4 and 4/4 musics. We can do interesting things rhythmically WITHIN a bar of music, or "over the barline" and through two or more measures of music (without playing beat "1" of each passing measure), by means of syncopation, hemiola, and accented sub-groupings.

Most of the rhythms you will encounter will be expressions of "2s + 3s," that is, rhythms made up of note values that equal 2 or 3 subdivisions. Perhaps without even realizing it, you have played many complex patterns of 2 + 3-note combinations. A good "conscious" and specific exercise to strengthen your knowledge and "gestalt"[9] of where beat "1" is at all times is to play the following rhythmic groupings in 4/4 time (a metronome with an accent-on-beat-one option is a good thing to have for this exercise); these first examples are relatively simple and straightforward.

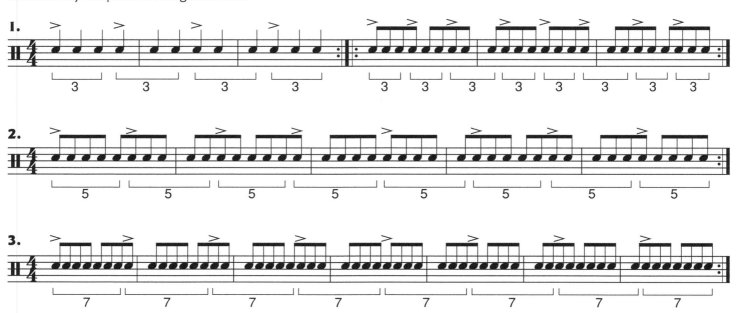

Another way to conceive or think of these types of rhythmic conundrums is to subgroup the "larger" groups of 5, 7, 9, etc., in smaller subdivisions of 2s + 3s.

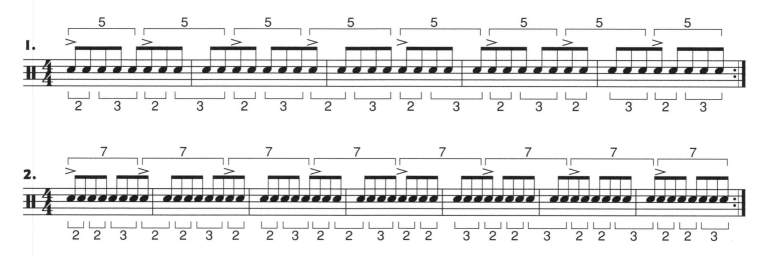

___

9   Perpetual awareness of structure and space.

These types of odd-and-even rhythmic groupings in 4/4 are not only the life blood of syncopated swing, they also suggest world music references. Some of these rhythms will sound familiar if you have listened to music from India or the African continent. They may also suggest sophisticated and complex contemporary music that is as yet unnamed—although Tony Williams brought such complexities into the world of jazz drumming back in the early 1960s with examples like these (from "Walkin'"—near end of the tenor solo from *Miles Davis in Europe)*:

Here is a fascinating rhythmic example. Taking the subdivision of 3-3-2 with an accent at the beginning of each group, you'll notice that the phrase sounds very much like the "Charleston" rag rhythm (or a Brazilian baião).

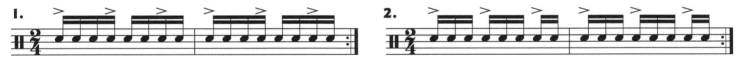

Now, instead of treating this rhythm in duple fashion, let's have some fun and utilize the grouping as a series of accented triplets (eighth-note triplets in 4/4 time):

Tricky!

Ravi Shankar, the famed Indian musician, composer and master of the sitar, showed this devilishly clever rhythmic cycle to odd-meter pioneer Don Ellis.

Here is that same rhythm with more visual clues and explanatory tuplet markings:

Okay ... before we proceed any further, let's listen to a simple and delightful waltz, a tune in the *bona fide* time signature of 3/4 (and not superimposed on top of something else). On the performance track from my trio's *Badlands* CD (Fuzzy Music), I begin the tune on brushes and later switch over to sticks. Simplicity and openness are the key elements here, in addition to musicality.

Since we have been working in 4/4 and 3/4 meter, it would be a good time now to investigate the most versatile of compound meters: 12/8.

12/8 is a primary metric template for many world musics, and I would like to show you some subdivisions that appear in African drumming. A bell pattern common in many musics from the African continent (particularly from the country of Ghana) looks like this:

Here is that same bell pattern, subdivided in various possible groupings. Play the bell pattern with one hand while saying or tapping out the rhythmic sub-grouping:

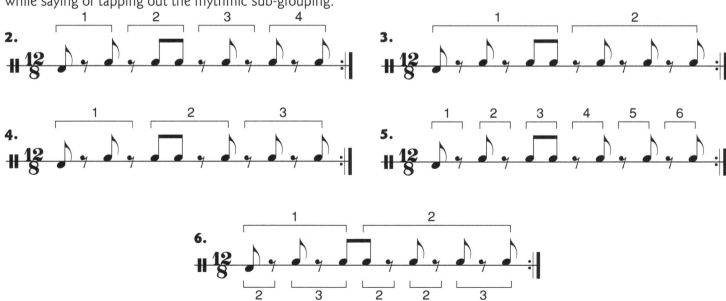

It is interesting how the same rhythm can feel so different, just by the natural emphasis that comes from each subdividing and grouping of the notes. It should be noted that in traditional African dance, the dancers prefer the grouping where the pattern is subdivided into four equal accents or parts. While examples **1 – 5** were all divided equally (groups of two, three, four notes, etc.), example **6** breaks the same-sounding phrase into an apparently complex combination of 5/8 + 7/8, subdivided 2-3 2-2-3.

If this is beginning to sound Greek to you, then good, because that's where we're going …

5/4

The Dave Brubeck Quartet's recording of Paul Desmond's composition "Take Five" changed modern music for good in the early 1960s:

As you can see, the song is built around a 5/4 pattern that basically equals one bar of 3/4 plus one bar of 2/4 (i.e., the feeling of a measure = a jazz waltz plus two beats).

Joe Morello's melodic, technically perfect, and rhythmically challenging solo changed **me** for good. Morello, thanks to his innate musicianship, intelligence, and practice (the band probably woodshedded the odd-time meter music fairly religiously) enabled him to go from this...

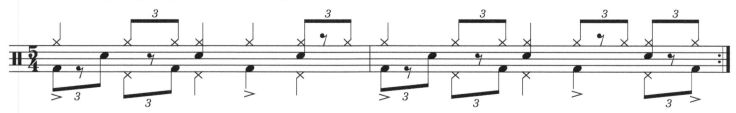

...to all sorts of variations, both in his timekeeping as well as in his extended solo. Familiarity breeds a musical comfort zone, as well as the ability to play several bars of 5/4 or 7/8 or 33/16 without having the need to play "1" on the downbeat of each bar with the bass drum! Actually, I suspect that Mr. Morello had a natural gift for polyrhythms and this type of music.

2 + 3 = 5

Basic math teaches us that 3 + 2 also equals 5, and so does 1 + 1 + 1 + 1 + 1.

Likewise, you can play 5/4 as:

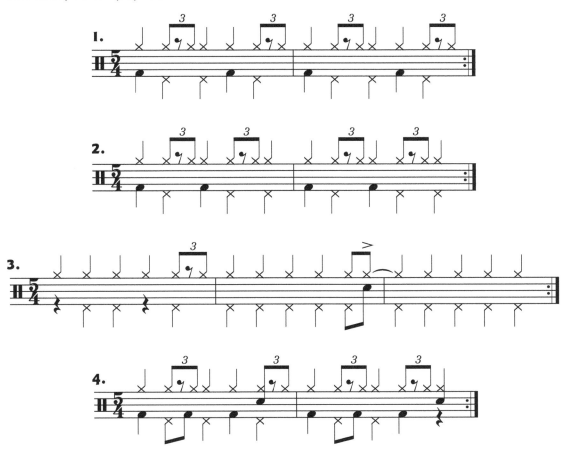

The three-pulse part of the measure can be played in the following ways:

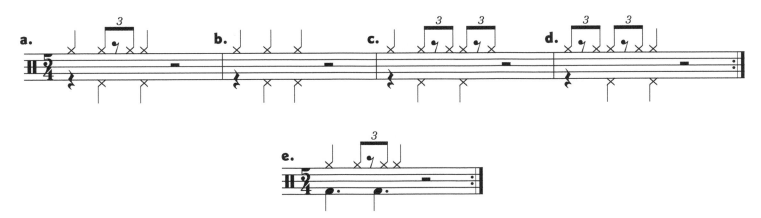

a.   ting-ting-a-ting

b.   ting-ting-ting (walk)

c.   1 + 2 subdivision

d.   2 + 1 subdivision

e.   dupled (turned into
     two dotted quarter notes)

When playing odd-time meters in most jazz music, the three-pulse part of the bar will often be dupled while the two-pulse part will be walked.

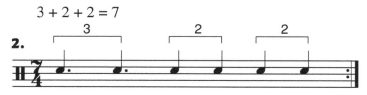

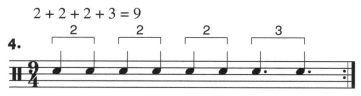

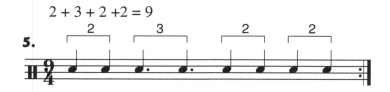

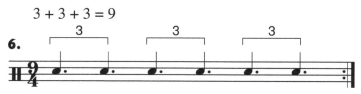

3 + 3 + 3 = 9

If the tempo is very fast, you can count or think of the various 2s and 3s as short and long. Trumpeter, composer, bandleader and musical visionary Don Ellis pioneered the use of odd-time signatures further than anyone else I can think of—to the extent, even, of writing one song that had 172 beats per bar! The term "odd" did not mean that the meters were "strange or weird, but rather that they are derived from odd numbers: 5, 7, 9, 11, 13, etc."[10]

Don Ellis, 1934 – 1978

The way Don Ellis figured it, if a song in 9 of folk-music origin from Turkey or Greece felt natural in a subdivision scheme of 2-2-2-3, then it would "then be possible to play in meters of even longer length, and this led to the development of such meters as 3-3-2-2-2-1-2-2-2 (19)."[11]

---

10   Don Ellis, *The New Rhythm Book*, Ellis Music Enterprises, 1972 p. 11. Sadly, this book is now out of print.

11   Ibid, p. 6

Here is the metric basis for a song that was brought into Don's band by Bulgarian pianist and composer Milcho Leviev. Based on a folk tune, this rhythm cycle contains 33 beats to the bar—and the way those guys played it, it swung!

As Don Ellis explained (and how the Ellis Band and Stan Kenton Orchestra composer Hank Levy taught me), it is often easier to think of the various 2s and 3s in terms of "short" and "long" as opposed to trying to count each beat. At a fast tempo, that would be impossible ("Because the pattern is so fast, it's almost like memorizing a melody, only in this case you are memorizing the feel of a rhythm. Usually the longs [3s] are stressed"). [12]

While 33/16 sounds sexy, 33/8 is an easier meter to notate and read. Here is a drumming pattern suggested by long-time Ellis drummer (and noted educator) Ralph Humphrey for the tune "Bulgarian Bulge," also known as "Bulgarian Boogie,"

Fun! Practice this, concentrate, and you'll be swinging in 33 in no time! [13]

Inspired by such rhythmic possibilities as well as by the haunting sound and ethos of Bulgarian choral music, I decided to try my hand at writing a piece of music in this style. Improvising the rhythmic and chordal scheme at the piano, I intuitively came up with something that sounded "ethnic" in odd-time, but proved in reality to work itself out in good old 6/4. I titled the tune "Bulgaria" and I have recorded this with my piano trios as well as with the WDR Big Band in Cologne, Germany.

The tune sounds for the most part as if it is written in some form of "5." Notice the various groupings of 2s and 3s that suggest this:

Combining the odds and evens within a framework of 6/4 seemed to give the song its best chance for swinging. Here is a piano lead-sheet of "Bulgaria."

---

12   Ibid, p.46
13   The two best-known drummers to have worked with Don Ellis were the late Steve Bohannon (probably one of the greatest drummers I have ever heard) and the great Ralph Humphrey. They could breathe fire and a complete sense of naturalness into this music. I recommend you find some Don Ellis big band recordings and check them out.

Bulgaria

Track 13

Peter Erskine

FREE IMPROVISATION . . .

This version of "Bulgaria" is from the *Live at Rocco* album I made with Alan Pasqua and Dave Carpenter. When improvising on top of a rhythmic structure such as this, your options include "catching" all or most of the rhythmic subdivisions, playing in rhythmic counterpoint, or playing over the larger form of the rhythm, i.e., in a more sweeping 6/4. The idea when playing ANY type of meter or beat is to "see" and "hear" the big picture; listening is the easiest way to do this.

The improvisation on this recording is in 4/4 (more or less). The open drum solo is actually one of my favorites; I was inspired that night by good friend Vinnie Colaiuta's presence at the gig! I hope you can hear and enjoy some of the thematic development, tension-and-release devices and general drum "schtuff" (as my father used to say).[14]

RECOMMENDED BOOKS

Modern Reading Text in 4/4 by Louie Bellson and Gil Breines
Published by Alfred Publishing Co., Inc.

Odd Time Reading Text by Louie Bellson and Gil Breines
Published by Alfred Publishing Co., Inc.

Even in the Odds by Ralph Humphrey
Published by C.L. Barnhouse Publications.

The Drum Perspective by Peter Erskine
Pubished by Hal Leonard Corporation

Effortless Mastery by Kenny Werner
Published by Jamey Abersold

Self-Portrait of a Jazz Artist by Dave Liebman
Published by Caris Music Services

Factorial Rhythm for All Instruments by Mick Goodrick and Mitch Haupers
Published by Mr. Goodchord Publications

---

14   An additional version of this song can be heard on my ECM album *Time Being*, as well as the Fuzzy Music compilation *Behind Closed Doors, Vol. 1* where I play a big band arrangement of the tune by Bill Dobbins with the WDR Big Band and guest vibraphonist Mike Mainieri.

RECOMMENDED STUDY AND PRACTICE METHODS FOR ODD-TIME MUSIC

In *The New Rhythm Book*, author Don Ellis outlines an exercise regimen that is very useful towards becoming more comfortable with odd-time meters. It involves the use of clapping the subdivisions, as well as counting the subdivisions (such as "1-2-3, 1-2, 1-2" for a measure of 7/4)[15]. He then instructs the student to both clap and count together:

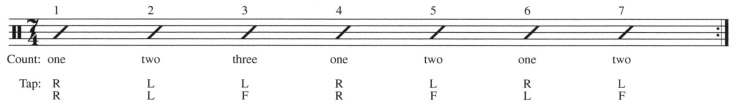

"The next exercise becomes slightly more difficult, because now we are going to count in double speed against the original claps using the subdivision 3-2-2. Keep the claps as in the single speed (above), and when that becomes comfortable then double the count against the single-speed claps!"

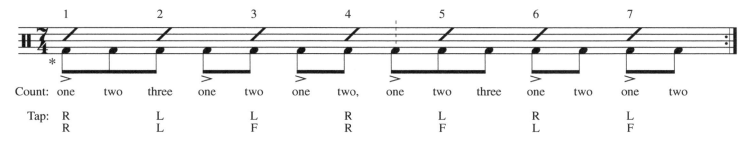

"Now you're really learning to execute and feel two separate rhythms at once. Your hands are clapping a 7/4[15] and you are reciting two 7/8s against the original 7/4. When you can do this you've broken the time barrier ..."[16]

You can use this technique with any metric challenge in terms of time signatures. Thinking and getting comfortable in two levels of rhythmic awareness works as well in 4/4 as it does in 13/8.

In the same book, pianist Milcho Leviev offers the following insight into how he and his fellow musicians on the Ellis band AND fellow musicians in Bulgaria treat subdivisions and their accents: While the tendency with any subdivision at first is to emphasize the downbeats of each subdivided group, the music will oftentimes swing or rock more if the concept below is observed.

When dealing with groupings of 2s and 3s, the "3" subdivision will be accented more heavily,

and the "3" group will be further subdivided in the form of an emphasis or heavy accent on the second or third note of the threes:

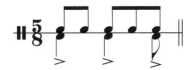   or

---

15   I have taken the liberty of adding the right foot to these exercises- P.E.
16   Don Ellis, The New Rhythm Book, Ellis Music Enterprises, 1972, p.20

"In the latter, the third accent sometimes is the heaviest one:

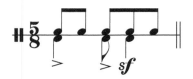

But the feeling still is 2+3, not 3+2! That's one of the secrets of how to play this music. We have something similar in jazz or rock when we accent the second and fourth beat in a 4/4 measure, and we never get lost, we feel the downbeat..."[17]

Good advice. An additional bit of wisdom from Mr. Ellis: "Singing is very important, because if you cannot sing a phrase and feel it correctly, there is no way you will be able to play it on your instrument. I find that if you keep practicing in this manner, progress comes relatively quickly."[18] The point of this is that it is possible and beneficial to practice AWAY from the drumset. Musical understanding comes from more than the mere movement of the hands.

Despite the complexities of much of the Ellis library of music, Don was a gifted melodist as well as rhythmic guru, and he composed some tremendously heartfelt music. I close this part of the book with one more quote from Don Ellis: "Among the most difficult things to do well in music are to really swing, and to compose or improvise a beautiful, simple melody. I maintain it is much easier to write or play a lot of fast notes which may appear to be very difficult but probably have little depth of meaning, than to do something really simple and beautiful, which is at the same time new and fresh."[19]

Let's return to our old friend Old MacDonald, now in 7/8 time. The metric subdivision is, for the most part, 2-2-3; however, bars 4, 8 + 12 are constructed using a 3-2-2 scheme. It is much easier to play a piece of music that's written in an odd time meter when you know the metric subdivision for each bar.

Bars 11 + 12, by the way, are a bit tricky because of the tied note between them. For more fun with this type of rhythmic elision (an elision is the perception of a metrically weak final chord or melody note as being in a strong position), see "On The Lake" (pp.60-61) and note its melody, which is almost entirely off-beat.

Taking rhythmic displacement one step further, see how easily you can play or sing "Old MacDonald's Far Out." To the ear, the melodic rhythm sounds like any old "Old MacDonald," but to the performer, it all sounds "off." It can take tremendous concentration to be able to maintain one's place in written music when the ear is begging us to differ. This is something that I've run into with classical music, particularly with the music of Igor Stravinsky and Leonard Bernstein.

Amen.

17   Don Ellis, *The New Rhythm Book*, Ellis Music Enterprises, 1972, pp.89-90
18   Ibid, p.14
19   Ibid, p.87

Old MacDonald in 7

Traditional

ON THE LAKE Track 14

Peter Erskine

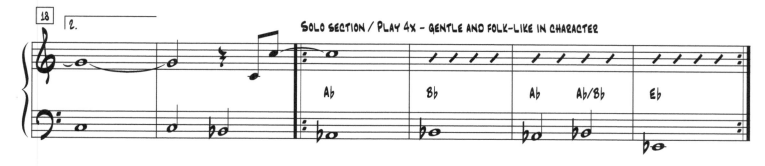

Last x Fine

Solo section / Play 4x – gentle and folk-like in character

Ab   Bb   Ab   Ab/Bb   Eb

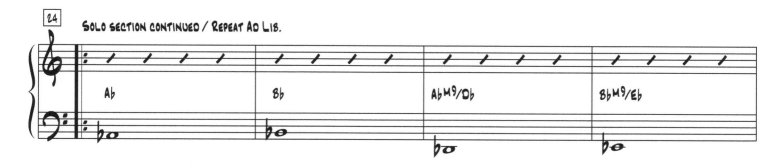

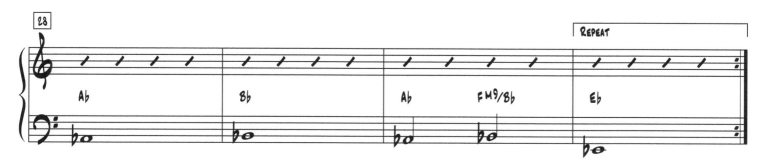

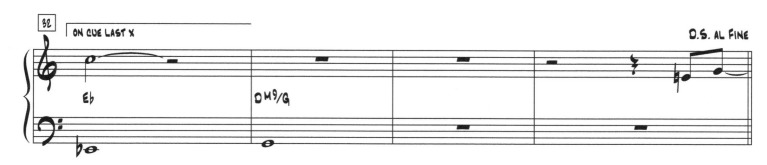

Old MacDonald's Far Out

Traditional

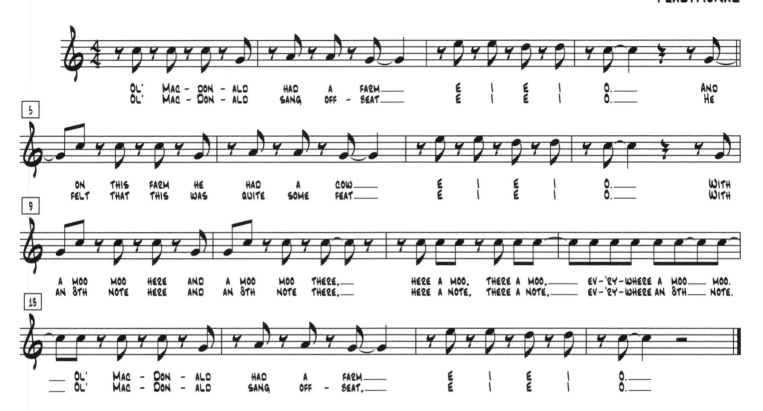

Quick'n
(Quartet)

 Track 16

Peter Erskine

Tempo range ♩ = 120-180

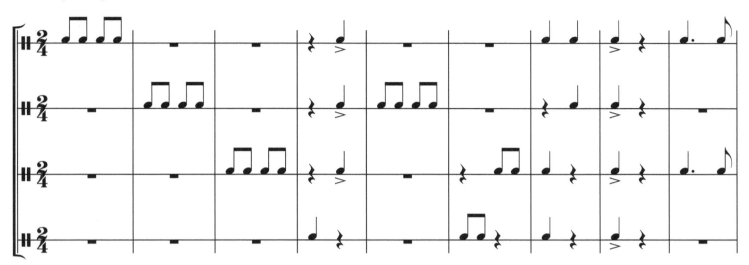

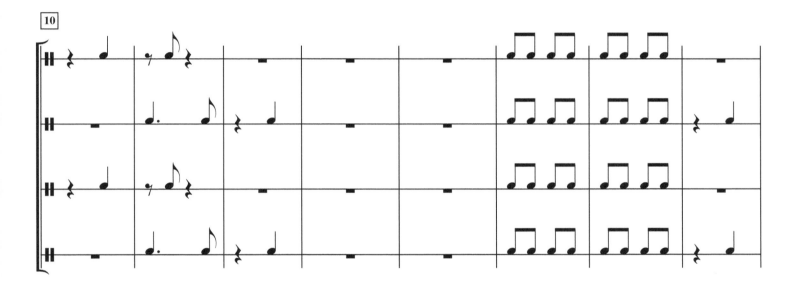

Quartet 4 the End of Time

 Track 17

Peter Erskine

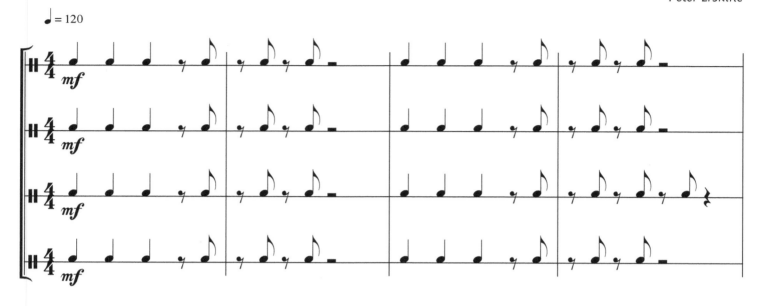

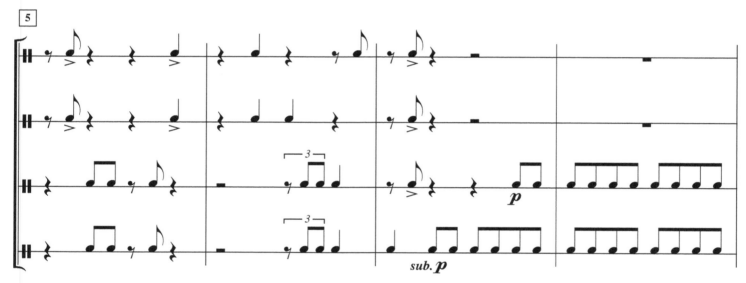

al' Hemiola Quartet Track 18

Peter Erskine

♩ = 120-180

Rhythm Quartet Track 19

Peter Erskine

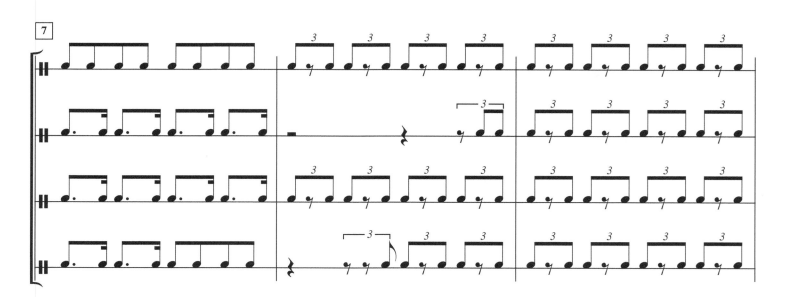

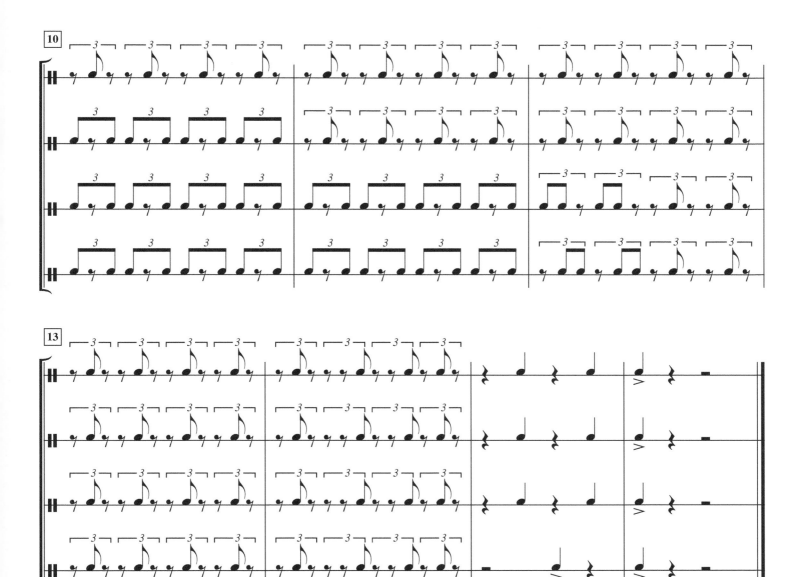

A suggested ABC of listening:

A. Louie Armstrong, Cannonball Adderly, John Abercrombie, Chet Atkins, Alex Acuña, AC/DC

B. Count Basie, **Art Blakey**, Gary Burton, **James Brown**, The Beatles, Richard Bona, The Band, The Beach Boys, The Brecker Brothers, Bob Berg, Louie Bellson, **Johann Sebastian Bach**, Johannes Brahms, **Ludwig van Beethoven**, Hector Berlioz, **Béla Bartók**, **Leonard Bernstein**, Samuel Barber, Benjamin Britten

C. John Coltrane, **Chick Corea**, **Ornette Coleman**, Ron Carter, **Ray Charles**, Nat King Cole, King Curtis, Michel Colombier, Aaron Copland, John Cage

D. Miles Davis, Bob Dylan, Jack DeJohnette, Palle Danielsson, George Duvivier, **Claude Debussy**, Frederick Delius

E. Duke Ellington, **Bill Evans**, Earth Wind & Fire, Eliane Elias, Peter Erskine, Marty Ehrlich, Edward Elgar

F. Ella Fitzgerald, Maynard Ferguson, Bill Frisell, **Aretha Franklin**, Roberta Flack

G. Stan Getz, Dexter Gordon, **Dizzy Gillespie**, Benny Goodman, Don Grolnick, Jan Garbarek, Johnny Griffin, George Garzone, **Jerry Goldsmith**

H. Coleman Hawkins, **Herbie Hancock**, **Freddie Hubbard**, **Roy Haynes**, Woody Herman, Charlie Haden, Donny Hathaway, Georg Frederic Handel, Bernard Herrmann

I. Charles Ives

J. Elvin Jones, **Keith Jarrett**, **Thad Jones/Mel Lewis Big Band**, **Antonio Carlos Jobim**, Philly Joe Jones, Papa Jo Jones, Osie Johnson, Marc Johnson

K. Stan Kenton, Diana Krall, Gene Krupa, B.B. King, Erich Wolfgang Korngold, Oliver Knussen

L. Don Lamond, Joe Lovano, Dave Liebman, The Lounge Art Ensemble, Little Feat, Will Lee, Nguyen Le, Magnus Lindberg

M. Charles Mingus, **Thelonius Monk**, Shelly Manne, John McGlaughlin, Pat Metheny, Christian McBride, Gary McFarland, Mike Mainieri, Joni Mitchell, Vince Mendoza, **Motown**, Sergio Mendes, Henry Mancini, Etienne Mbappe, **The Meters**, Paul Motian, Wynton & Branford Marsalis, Brad Mehldau, Bob Mintzer Big Band, **Wolfgang Amadeus Mozart**, Gustav Mahler, Ennio Morricone

N. Oliver Nelson, Milton Nascimento

O. Claus Ogerman, Anita O'Day, Arturo "Chico" O'Farrell, Shuggie Otis, Darek Oles

P. Charlie Parker, Oscar Peterson, Oscar Pettiford, Bernard "Pretty" Purdie, **Jaco Pastorius**, John Patitucci, Prince, Alan Pasqua, Chris Potter, Henry Purcell, Sergei Prokofiev, Giacomo Puccini

Q. Queen Latifah

R. Sonny Rollins, **Buddy Rich**, **Max Roach**, Chuck Rainey, Elis Regina, The Rolling Stones, Sergei Rachmaninoff, Nikolai Rimsky-Korsakov, Maurice Ravel, Miklos Rosza

S. Wayne Shorter, **Frank Sinatra**, **John Scofield**, Jimmy Smith, Sly & the Family Stone, Steely Dan,

Mike Stern, Billy Stewart, Boz Scaggs, Franz Schubert, Robert Schuman, **Igor Stravinsky**, Dmitri Shostakovitch, Richard Strauss, Max Steiner, Karlheinz Stockhausen, Esa-Pekka Salonen

T. Art Tatum, Grady Tate, McCoy Tyner, John Taylor, **Tower of Power**, Richard Tee, Toto, Piotr Tchaikovsky, Toru Takemitsu, Mark-Anthony Turnage

U. Union Station w/ Alison Krauss

V. Sarah Vaughn, Miroslav Vitous, **Edgar Varése**, Ralph Vaughn-Williams

W. Chick Webb, Ben Webster, **Weather Report**, **Tony Williams**, Kenny Wheeler, Kenny Werner, Joe Williams, Jeff "Tain" Watts, Patrick Williams, William Walton, John Williams

X. Iannis Xenakis

Y. Lester Young, Yellowjackets, Larry Young

Z. Joe Zawinul, Frank Zappa

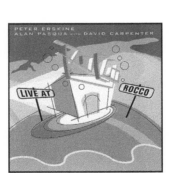

Final Thoughts

Author and inventor Ray Kurzweil notes in his book *The Age of Spiritual Machines*: "We regard time as moving in one direction because processes in time are not generally reversible. If we smash a cup, we find it difficult to unsmash it. The reason for this has to do with the second law of thermodynamics. Since overall entropy may increase but can never decrease, time has directionality. Smashing a cup increases randomness. Unsmashing the cup would violate the second law of thermodynamics." By the way, Kurzweil defines "entropy" as "a term to describe the extent of randomness and disorder of a system." The Laws of Thermodynamics, meanwhile, "govern how and why energy is transferred."

This photo of myself and the statue of Ludwig van Beethoven was taken in the lobby of the Vienna Konzerthaus. Whether you play jazz, funk, folk, rock or classical (I like to play all of these types of music, and then some!), your enjoyment will be more profound when you can play with rhythmic gusto and confidence. I hope that the studies in this book will help you towards that goal.

William Shakespeare's Hamlet provides us with one more instructional bit of fun that you can try with your fellow musical colleagues, and it goes like this: gather nine (or less) other musicians and position yourselves in a circle. Taking the opening lines of the play's best-known soliloquy, "To be or not to be, that is the question," split the verse up so that each word is spoken by one person in the circle ... continue round until the phrase is complete. You will notice that, even if each person speaking recites their word in "perfect" time or rhythm, the overall effect is probably not "music to your ears". You can only hope to form a "musical" phrase by listening intently to the word being "played" by the musician next to you (or, before and after), and so on. Even though rhythm is an absolute, it needs the elements of dynamics, tone, inflection and musical judgement to render it "musical." Earlier in the book, the question is asked: "Why does music make our hearts soar?" The answer? Because it touches our souls. How does it do this? I'm still trying to figure that one out.

"I despise a world which does not feel that music is a higher revelation than all wisdom and philosophy."
— Ludwig van Beethoven

"Another thing about rhythm is that when an artist is performing on his instrument he breathes in his normal fashion. When the artist is breathing improperly, it's like the audience is left with a little case of indigestion. It's like eating a meal in a hurry. **Not swinging** is like that. It leads to tension in the audience. It's a physical reaction which you give off." — "Papa" Jo Jones

"I was taught by Chick Webb that, if you're playing before an audience, you're supposed to take them away from everyday life — wash away the dust of everyday life. And that's all music is supposed to do."
— Art Blakey

"There is nothing to it. You only have to hit the right note at the right time, and the instrument plays itself."
— Johann Sebastian Bach

CD Track Listing

1.   **Drum Fanfare/Fable**

2.   **Sax and Drums Improvisation**

3.   **I Could Write A Book**

4.   **I Could Write A Book w/ click**

5.   **Sideman Bop**

6.   **Jazz 4/4 Time (drums) ***

7.   **Rhythm Method ***

8.   **Rock/Pop Feel (drums) ***

9.   **Family Fun(k) ***

10.   **16th-Note Groove (drums) ***

11.   **The Cats ***

12.   **Summer's Waltz**

13.   **Bulgaria**

14.   **On the Lake**

15.   **Sweet Soul ***

16.   **Quick'n**

17.   **Quartet 4 The End Of Time**

18.   **al' Hemiola Quartet**

19.   **Rhythm Quartet**

* No written examples included

About the Recordings

DRUM FANFARE/FABLE
From: History of the DRUM (PEPCD100), courtesy of Fuzzy Music (fuzzymusic.com)
Recitation: Roscoe Lee Browne
Recorded at Skyline Studios, New York, NY & Pacifique Studios, N. Hollywood, CA
Engineered by James Farber & Ken Deranteriasian
Text by Jack Fletcher, drum solo composed by Peter Erskine (Ersko Music)

SAX/DRUMS IMPROVISATION & I COULD WRITE A BOOK
Tenor Saxophone: Gilad Ronen
Recorded at Puck Productions, Santa Monica, CA
Engineered by Peter Erskine

SIDEMAN BOP
From: Side Man Blue (PEPCD010), courtesy of Fuzzy Music (fuzzymusic.com)
Trumpet: Andy Haderer
Tenor Saxophone: Rölf Römer
Piano: Frank Chastenier
Bass: John Goldsby
Recorded at WDR Studio 4, Cologne, Germany
Engineered by Reinholdt Nickel

RHYTHM METHOD
From: You Call This A Living? (WB-1002), courtesy of Wag Wecords
Leader/Trumpet Soloist: Wayne Bergeron
Trumpets and flugelhorns: Warren Luening, Rick Baptist, Dennis Farias, Larry Hall, Deborah Wagner
Trombones: Charlie Loper, Andy Martin, Bruce Otto, Bill Reichenbach
Saxophones: Dan Higgins, Greg Huckins (alto & flute); Bill Liston & Jeff Driskill (tenor & flute); Jay Mason (baritone & flute)
Piano: Alan Pasqua
Bass: Chuck Berghofer
Drums: Peter Erskine
Executive Producer: Gary Grant
Assoc. Producers: Andy Waterman, Wayne Bergeron
Recorded at The Bakery Digital Sound and Vision, Pasadena, CA
Additional tracking: Bluebell Studios & Valerio Sound
Engineered by Andy Waterman
Mixed by: Andy Waterman, Gary Grant, Wayne Bergeron
Mastered by: Damon A. Tedesco of Mobile DISC & D.A.T.
Musician contractor: Deborah Wagner
Music prep: Tom Kubis, Bill Liston
Composed & arranged by Tom Kubis

FAMILY FUN(K)
Piano: Alan Pasqua
Guitar: Grant Geissman
Bass: Dave Carpenter
Recorded at Puck Productions, Santa Monica, CA
Engineered by Dan Pinder
Composed by Peter Erskine (Ersko Music)

THE CATS
From: Gun Smith Cats (Soundtrack)
Piano: Russell Ferrante
Guitar: Bob Mann
Bass: Will Lee
L.A. Horn Section, arranged and conducted by Vince Mendoza
Recorded at Oceanway Studios, Hollywood, CA
Engineered by Malcom Pollack
Composed by Peter Erskine (Ersko Music)

SUMMER'S WALTZ & ON THE LAKE
From: Badlands (PEPCD011), courtesy of Fuzzy Music (fuzzymusic.com)
Piano: Alan Pasqua
Bass: Dave Carpenter
Recorded at Puck Productions, Santa Monica, CA
Engineered by Brian Risner
Mixed by Rich Breen

BULGARIA
From: Live at Rocco (PEPCD007), courtesy of Fuzzy Music (fuzzymusic.com)
Piano: Alan Pasqua
Bass: Dave Carpenter
Recorded "live" and mixed by Rich Breen

SWEET SOUL (this is an excellent example of how to play a slow tempo!)
From: Sweet Soul (PEPCD006), courtesy of Fuzzy Music (fuzzymusic.com)
Guitar: John Scofield
Tenor Saxophone: Bob Mintzer
Tenor Saxophone: Joe Lovano
Trumpet: Randy Brecker
Piano/Organ: Kenny Werner
Bass: Marc Johnson
Recorded at Skyline Studios, New York, NY
Engineered by James Farber
Composed by Peter Erskine (Ersko Music)

SOLO DRUMMING & RHYTHM QUARTETS
Recorded at Puck Productions, Santa Monica, CA.

All drum tracks performed by Peter Erskine.